THE COPYWRITER'S GUIDE TO GETTING PAID:

How To Land Awesome Clients And Earn A Great Living As A Copywriter

ROY FURR

The Copywriter's Guide to Getting Paid

Publishing support, design, and composition by:
90-Minute Books
Newinformation Inc
302 Martinique Drive
Winter Haven, FL 33884
www.90minutebooks.com

ISBN-13:978-1515215967
ISBN-10:1515215962

For more information on 90-Minute Books including finding out how you can
publish your own lead generating book, visit www.90minutebook.com or call
(863) 318-0464

Here's What's Inside...

Foreword

I guess you can call me a "wannabe" when it comes to copywriting... That is, I wish I could write as well as the folks I've hired and worked with in my 30+ year career in direct response marketing.

But I know I can't... And I know the value of hiring someone with this incredible skill set... And I know it's game changing for any business to hire the right copywriter for the right project.

I am very proud to say that I have worked with the world's best... From Gene Schwartz to Gary Bencivenga to Bill Jayme to Clayton Makepeace to Jim Rutz (and of course now I have insulted all of the other top copywriters who probably won't write for me anymore now)!

But seriously, what I've learned working with the best of the best is that they didn't get there by accident... They all needed guidance, training and mentoring, often from folks who were far too busy to "teach" because they were writing all the time.

Roy Furr is a guy who is committed to teaching AND writing... And I believe a book like this is the perfect first step to take your career to the next level.

Will you be ready for an assignment from me after reading this book?

Probably not.

But will you be able to get to the next level without the kind of training Roy is giving you here?

Definitely not.

And don't get me wrong: as a direct marketer always looking for creative talent, I am not an elitist... Just cautious... Because I know that the cost of hiring someone who is not up to snuff is much higher than paying a top copywriter huge amounts of money whether that top copywriter wins OR loses.

So how does a newbie really break in?

First, read this book... Roy understands what it takes to get noticed, what it takes to get read, and what it takes to get your first assignment.

And it is NOT an "easy button." It takes time, effort, research diligence, study... All of the things I write about regularly and all the things Roy writes about regularly... Much of which is featured in this book.

Just recently, I tried my hand at writing a sales letter for a live event I was planning... The event was very personal, I knew everything I wanted to say, and after 30 years in direct response marketing and working with all of those superstars, how tough could it be?

It was tough.

After writing 7 or 8 pages over 7 or 8 hours I sent what I had written to one of those world class copywriters — one that I didn't name drop above — and he basically told me what a wonderful direct marketer I am... But that I should clearly hire a copywriter.

I hired Roy to build on what I had written and he made it sing... In my voice too! It led to a super-successful letter for that event, a letter even the great Gary Bencivenga was impressed with... And

Gary was profiled in the letter (he was a speaker at the event)!

I knew right then and there that Roy was a copywriter who understood the business (as much as he understood me); and it's why he's been able to be as successful as he's become in a very competitive industry at such a young age.

And when I heard he was putting together this book to share all the career-building lessons for copywriters he has learned to date, it's clear that he is not just a great copywriter but now an industry leader as well.

You have made a great decision to buy this book... But now the work is only beginning.

If you treat this book like you use the snack bar at your gym (where you insist you are still "working out"), Roy's advice won't be enough...

However, if you are taking action on everything Roy tells you to do, you won't regret it... And you will be on your way to "getting paid"... And the riches will be far beyond just money.

Brian Kurtz

Serial Direct Marketer, Past Executive VP at Boardroom Inc., and founder of Titans Marketing LLC

Introduction

In 2005, I discovered the world of freelance copywriting. And in the decade since then, I've managed to become one of the best-known up-and-coming copywriters in the direct response world. (I say up-and-coming because my career is nothing compared to MY heroes — even though many in the industry now look up to me.)

Along the way, I've had an interesting and unique journey. While I went through many of the same struggles as we all do — trying to make sense of the opportunity, figuring out how to get clients, and how to get paid and turn it into a full-time income — I also got a different perspective on the industry.

Due to some early success, I was quickly writing about copywriting for AWAI (the copywriter training company) and others. I was brought into the inner sanctum of direct marketing, and got to know many top direct marketers. I took on roles where I hired and fired copywriters; all while going through my own successes and failures as an early-career copywriter.

This has given me a multi-dimensional perspective on the industry: as an insider, in the trenches with you, just trying to make this copywriting thing work out; as a client, working with copywriters; and as a 3rd party observer, watching with a journalist's perspective, seeing how the industry worked and what made the successful copywriters that way.

I know the doubts. I know the fears. I know the frustrations. But I also know the successes, the wins and big achievements.

All of this adds up to a unique take on the industry. And specifically what it takes to get ahead and get paid — to turn your knowledge of copywriting into a great living as a copywriter.

What you're about to read is the edited transcript of an interview I did with Susan Austin, covering some of the most important concepts you need to know about landing awesome clients and earning a great living as a copywriter.

Following the interview is a series of articles from my site, Breakthrough Marketing Secrets, at **http://www.BreakthroughMarketingSecrets.com.** These articles were hand-selected out of hundreds of articles on the site as the most important things I think you need to know if you want to get started earning a substantial living as a copywriter.

This is not a book designed to teach you copywriting itself — although there are many pointers that will help you write the most valuable copy for your clients. Rather, it's a book that I think fills a very real gap in the education of many folks who are getting going in their copywriting careers — how to turn all that "how to" knowledge into real cash in your bank account. And not only how to get paid today, but the strategies you want to use to earn a great income for the rest of your career as a copywriter.

Yours for bigger breakthroughs,

Roy Furr

THE COPYWRITER'S GUIDE TO GETTING PAID

How to Start at Zero and Become a Successful Copywriter

Susan: Good afternoon, this is Susan Austin, and I'm super excited to be here with acclaimed direct response copywriter Roy Furr. Roy is going to be sharing his thoughts and ideas on how copywriters can land awesome clients and earn a great living. Welcome, Roy.

Roy: Thank you, Susan. I'm excited. Thank you for being here and for interviewing me.

Susan: So, Roy, let's start at the beginning. What got you into copywriting?

Roy: If you go all the way back to before I knew what copywriting was, I was working at the local gas company in their customer service call center.

If you were one of those people who didn't pay your bill all winter and you let the bills keep stacking up, eventually we'd come out on that first warm day of spring and shut off your service. And I was the guy you would call and YELL AT because we shut off your gas service. It was a pretty horrible job.

There were good parts and bad parts, but overall it was not a very fulfilling job for someone like me.

What it allowed me to do though, was read a lot in between calls. And I read a few books which turned me on to copywriting and marketing.

I didn't have a marketing background. I did have an undergraduate degree in psychology — which had only qualified me for that horrible customer service job. I didn't have any connections. I had zero experience, and there was no good reason anybody should hire me for a marketing job.

However, once I discovered copywriting and direct response marketing, I knew it was for me. I started applying for marketing jobs, and I would say, "You don't have any good reason to hire me just from looking at my resume. I don't have the level of experience other applicants will have. But I do have a ton of ambition and a willingness to do what it takes to be successful."

This is how I got my first marketing job, and I worked my butt off for that company, and I created some very solid successes by learning on the job.

We landed the company on Inc. Magazine's list of America's fastest growing private companies. We more than doubled the business. We did better than that in profits. The owner bought the most expensive house in the city as the result of the success we created.

It all came out of my willingness to start from nothing and do what it would take to be successful.

Susan: Was that first marketing job a copywriting position Roy?

Roy: It wasn't exclusively copywriting. It wasn't even for a traditional "direct marketing" company. A large portion of my work was copywriting, and I got to practice and hone my skills there. But I did a lot more.

I took over for the guy who ran it before, who had moved up to be the president of the company. I did everything from buying traffic, to updating the website, to sending out direct mail pieces, to writing product descriptions and running launches, to pulling customers' information out of the database. It was a very broad marketing education in a single job.

Susan: So how did you get started with freelance copywriting?

Roy: While I was employed at that marketing job, I also started freelancing in the early mornings and late at night.

I had the desire to be a freelancer from the very beginning. But I also wanted to succeed in the job, because I knew it would get me from point A to point B; and allow me to have a solid income while I continued to learn.

So I did both at the same time, making the scheduling work to fit the two.

At first, it was tough. I was completely terrified of getting my first clients, and I didn't really know what to do. I didn't know how to be successful in doing a copywriting project with a client. I didn't know how to be successful doing any of it! But I moved forward anyway and learned as I went. And it wasn't always easy, but I started to create some successes.

The success I created on the side allowed me to launch my freelance career full-time in February 2010, which was also a really scary endeavor. I was my family's primary income earner, and I was giving up a rock solid salary and performance bonuses for the great unknown of freelancing. Not only that, we had a mortgage and a new kid less than one year old.

It came down to me not having any choice but to be successful. And so I did what it took, starting that year...

A lot of folks in the copywriting world know AWAI. They are one of the world's leading trainers of copywriters. Every year AWAI singles out one person as the hottest up and coming direct response copywriter in the industry and gives them a $10,000 award. It's a big check awarded up on stage at their annual event.

In 2010, my first year as a full time freelancer, I won the AWAI $10K challenge award. I guess it was proof I was doing something right!

That helped build my reputation as an in-demand consultant and copywriter to direct response financial publishers and others.

Since then, I've worked hard to ensure the successes kept piling up...

I've written controls — the industry term for the most successful promotion in a test — and created profitable marketing campaigns for some of the biggest and best marketers in the business: InvestorPlace Media, Independent Living News, Mauldin Economics, Casey Research, Money Map Press, AWAI, Nightingale-Conant, Brian Tracy International, and others.

And recently I wrote a very exciting promotion for a seminar called The Titans of Direct Response, for Brian Kurtz at Boardroom, now Titans Marketing. It's one of the most widely-circulated promotions in our industry in recent times, because the event itself is probably the biggest direct marketing event of the decade. Not since Gary Bencivenga's retirement seminar has an event garnered as much industry attention.

(This once-in-a-lifetime event featured Dan Kennedy, Gary Bencivenga, Greg Renker, Jay Abraham, Ken McCarthy, Perry Marshall, Joe Sugarman, Fred Catona, Eric Betuel, David Deutsch, Arthur Johnson, Parris Lampropoulos, Michael Fishman, Jim Kwik, and Ryan Lee — plus Brian Kurtz. What a lineup!)

I hadn't taken on any client work outside the financial space in a long time. But when Brian came to me with that project, I really couldn't refuse.

That pretty much brings us up to today. And gives you some background as to where I come from as we walk through all of this — as we discuss how I was able to create the successes I had from starting out, knowing nothing, to becoming one of the best-known and most in-demand copywriters in the business.

What Type of Copywriting Pays Best?

Susan: What a journey! Well Roy, I know that some copywriters get paid quite well — and others, not so much. You've told me that it actually starts with the type of copywriting they choose. So can you tell me, what type of copywriting work pays best?

Roy: One of the biggest problems many aspiring copywriters have is choosing the wrong type of work. A lot of us come to this profession out of an interest in writing.

And if you're just interested in writing, you'll just want to do any kind of writing work you can get. However, there's a big difference between a blog post that's put on a website and a sales letter that does a million dollars in revenue.

I was glad I learned this early on, because it's helped me be far more successful throughout my entire career.

If you choose the wrong type of writing it can dramatically decrease your earnings potential. The good news is if you choose the right type it can dramatically increase your earnings potential, and it's not necessarily because of how good of a writer you are.

This really is the missing link to earning a great living as a writer. If you just want to write, you won't necessarily make a great living. But if you write to sell, then you can find incredible opportunities as a copywriter.

One of the things I emphasize to many different copywriters whom I speak with through my

Breakthrough Marketing Secrets website (www.BreakthroughMarketingSecrets.com) and elsewhere is you really do have to fall in love with selling.

Selling is not evil. It's about solving problems folks have and want to find a solution to. It's about fulfilling their desires and creating enjoyment in their life. What you need to know is you cannot manipulate or move people to take actions that they don't want to take.

The desire has to be there in the first place for you to make the sale. Then as the copywriter, you have to meet that desire or the problem with a compelling presentation of a product that fulfills their need or desire.

The biggest distinction when you ask what type of copywriting pays best is "how close to the sale" versus "how far from the sale" your writing is used.

If you're just writing content, for example for SEO — search engine optimization — or blog posts, you're far from the sale. Yes, it matters that you're driving traffic to the website, but it's inherently a far lower value to a company than being able to consistently bring new customers through the door or generate additional revenue from their past customers.

If your copy is actually making a financial transaction take place — if it's measurably creating revenue — then of course it's far more valuable. One hundred percent of the value you can create for a client is in driving the sale forward.

And that's why I fell in love with direct response copywriting as a field. It's the biggest income opportunity for copywriters, to be able to move the reader toward making that purchase.

When you can drive the sale itself, when you can get the customer to actually pull out their wallet and place their order, that's where the big money is. Because — like we're going to talk about here today — companies will pay you a sales person's commission, a royalty for the amount of sales that you make.

Susan: What is an example of copywriting that doesn't pay well?

Roy: One example is writing just to get readership — writing that does not ask for an action or move the customer closer to the sale. It can be a webpage, a blog post, or any other piece of content for content's sake.

As a writer, you shouldn't get into copywriting just because you want to write or just because you want to tell stories. All good direct response marketing moves the reader a measured distance toward the transaction. So your clients know how well your copy drove the reader toward the sale. They send out the sales letter and generate this many sales and this much revenue. That's how you'll be judged.

If you don't want to write that — if you want to write articles, or content-driven emails, or any number of pieces of writing that a company may use that don't push the reader any closer to buying the product — then those will always be lower paid positions than the writing that generates revenue. That's the big difference that determines how much you make as a copywriter.

How to Get Your First Copywriting Client

Susan: You said earlier you were terrified of having to get clients. How did you get your first client?

Roy: I was already working this full time marketing job, and I was following all these different folks in the marketing world. One particular guy's work jumped out at me.

His name is David Bullock, and he is one of the world's leading authorities on Taguchi testing for marketing, and a lot more these days. Taguchi is an advanced statistical model for running marketing tests that tends to only be used in very high volume marketing departments.

Before discovering David, I was already attracted to marketing testing. (The culture of testing happens to be one of my 9 Criteria of a Perfect Copywriting Client, explained in Appendix C in this book.)

Anyway, David was out there, and I decided, "Okay. I think I'd really like to work with David as my first freelance copywriting client." I had communicated with him by email and I think by phone a time or two beforehand, just casual emails.

But at some point I just had to turn around and say to myself, "Alright, it's time to get serious. I want him as a client."

I wrote David what I call an irresistible offer letter. In short, I made an offer to him which was very one-sided in his favor. It was so compelling that it was much easier for him to say yes than to say no. So I ended up getting the work. (In Appendix A in the back of the book, you'll find an article that includes

9

both the letter itself and my explanation of that process.)

I basically said, "I'd like to write something for you. If you don't like it, you don't have to test it at all, and you don't have to pay me. If you decide you want to test it, that's great. You still don't have to pay me if you test it and it doesn't work. If you decide you like it, AND you decide to test it, AND it does work — if it beats your current letter that you're using to sell this product — then in that case, here's the fee that I would like you to pay me."

He had nothing to lose.

David was only going to have to pay me if I increased his profits. Of course he was going to say yes to that.

I don't necessarily recommend this to get clients for somebody that's at the level where I'm at today. But it can work when you're starting out and you want to get that first client, or if you want to break into a new industry where you don't have experience.

This irresistible offer letter is an incredible way to do that because you make it so hard for them to say no that you are almost guaranteed to get a yes.

Susan: That's brilliant. Did you look for someone who had material that wasn't up to what you thought was good enough?

Roy: Yes, it was very much a case of him not being a copywriter, and he'll never tell you that he is a copywriter. He hadn't hired a copywriter to do the first letter, and so it wasn't that great.

I liked him because of the product, but it was definitely a situation where I could say, "I think I could do a better job than he did there." And yeah, I did exactly that, and the rest is history. He remains a good friend to this day, and we've done a few projects together, in fact.

Susan: So he hired you, and he paid your fee no problem?

Roy: Yes. I think to some degree you have to trust whomever you choose to reach out to if you're going to send a letter like that.

You have to trust they're going to be a person who will pay your fee. I certainly chose to reach out to someone with a high presence in the marketplace because it's harder to be at a high level in the marketplace if you are going to stiff all your service providers. I also had the general gut impression of him that he acted with integrity.

It worked out very well, and he paid my fee, and like I said, we went on to do more work together.

Should You Do Spec Work?

Susan: Another common opportunity for newer copywriters is "spec work." Do you recommend newer writers start out by doing spec assignments?

Roy: What I did was very similar to the kind of spec work that copywriters are asked to do quite often. That's basically to work on spec, which means I do the work first, and then if you like it, you pay me to complete it.

The difference between what I did with David and the standard spec assignments is that I went out and created my own spec assignment to get that client. I said, "I'll do this work. And if you like it, you pay me."

Within the copywriting world, and especially within the direct response copywriting world, there are a lot of clients who post to various job boards or internet forums or elsewhere that say largely the same thing.

"You do a little bit of work for us. You write the beginning of a sales letter. And if we like it we'll hire you to write the whole thing."

My answer to the question of "Should a copywriter do spec work?" is yes — but only specifically when you want to get started as a copywriter or to break into a new industry.

Your most important thing in getting started as a copywriter is to get experience and start working with clients. That's absolutely critical above everything else... Above creating a website, above figuring out how you're going to market yourself, above all of that.

Just get your first experience under your belt, and then your second and your third.

In getting started, yes you should do spec work. You should do anything to get experience.

You should also do spec work when you want to break into a new industry. I had this happen to me. I'd had a few years' success as a part-time freelancer, and then maybe eight months of success as a full-time freelancer. But not in the financial newsletter publishing industry, which is where I wanted to end up as a freelance copywriter.

So I found a good client who had posted a spec assignment out there saying, "Hey, we're looking for a new copywriter, and if you're interested do the spec assignment." And I took them up on it because I wanted to break into this new industry.

I didn't have experience or samples to show of actual work that had been done in that industry. And so instead I completed their spec assignment, and then I got the gig for the promo.

It started as a one-project contract. And that one-project contract was quickly followed by a three-project contract with that same client; followed by a monthly retainer, and I ended up working with them for about 18 months on an exclusive basis.

I wrote my first $1 million promo with a huge royalty payment to follow during the course of that engagement. All of that came out of that initial spec assignment.

Yeah, absolutely, as a new copywriter you should do spec work to get started, and any time you need to do it to break into a new industry.

But then you want to stop as soon as possible because continuing to do the spec assignments with every client in your industry is really bad for long-term positioning. At some point you want to be the copywriter who never has to do spec assignments because people know your work well enough. That is where you want to be long term.

But if you want to get paid in the short term, doing the spec assignments can be a fast path to get there.

Susan: Spec work doesn't pay as much as other work either — does it?

Roy: Yes and no. The way that it's set up is you don't get paid to do the first part of the project. You do enough so that they know how you're going to handle the project.

It's on spec, which is a common term in a few creative industries that means, "Hey, I'm going to create this. You're going to look at it, and then if you like it then you're going to pay me."

There's no guarantee of ANY income in doing it, but typically you're writing maybe a couple of pages, around a thousand words, something like that.

It's not a ton of work but it it's enough for the client to know whether or not you will be worth the investment.

But then the actual amount you get paid when you get the gig can be whatever works out for you and the client — it's not necessarily less.

For that first financial project, I think my fee was $4,000 total. Then there's royalty to be earned on top of that. In the months before that, I'd done other similar-sized projects for less than that. So once I got the gig, I was also getting a raise. It was definitely a case of the spec assignment getting me a higher fee than I'd been earning before.

Typically when you're getting into the industry, spec work or not, the fees aren't huge. You shouldn't expect that. But depending on the client, they may be higher than what you're getting right now.

You also have the potential to earn big royalties. If you follow my recommendations for how to set up your arrangements with clients, this will definitely be part of your contract. And if the promo you write as part of the spec assignment goes on to be successful, the royalties you earn could lead to a big payday.

And yet, even as I tell you that you can make a lot of money from a spec assignment, that's not how I think you should think about it. A spec assignment is about starting the relationship. And ideally you're trying to get into a client where the relationship can be quite valuable if you succeed. Or at least don't fall on your face too hard on that first project. Most clients are looking for folks that they can work with for the long term — and don't expect a home run on the first go. Especially from someone they hire through a spec assignment. They're looking to find someone they can work with for a long time, in a mutually-beneficial relationship.

How to Work with the Best Companies in the Industry

Susan: Now I know you've come a long way since your spec days. You're now working with some of the top clients in your field. How does someone go about following your path and working with the top companies in their given industry?

Roy: I've developed a reputation of having no problem getting in with a lot of the top companies in my industry. I have connections and a work history with some pretty incredible folks.

I can look back at where I was in 2005, when I first discovered copywriting... Or 2007, when I started taking on freelance work... Or even 2010, when I went full-time as a freelancer...

There were a lot of giants in the industry that I looked up to and thought, "Jeez, if I could ever work with those companies I would surely be a success." Now I've worked with many of them.

I think when a lot of folks get started in the industry they see these giants, these Titans as being almost impossible to get in with. I did too. Yet since then, I've added them all to my personal client list.

How'd that happen?

Over and over again, I've simply reached out to them to get connected; whether it's been a LinkedIn connection, a letter of introduction via email, or occasionally a letter of introduction via direct mail. Simple as that — I just reach out.

You can do whatever works for you. Just get connected, even if it seems hard to do at first. As soon as I hit send or put that letter in the mailbox or whatever, I am absolutely scared out of my mind about what the response is going to be. It's a completely terrifying experience, but I force myself to keep doing it, and I succeed anyway.

Keep in mind, these companies, especially the ones that have a process in place for hiring copywriters — the direct marketing companies — they need copywriters as much as you need clients.

They want to find the next great copywriter.

Because the person on staff that finds that next great copywriter — who is able to write a number of million dollar promotions and add all these new customers to the customer database — that person is getting the corner office. They're getting a bigger salary, they're getting more perks, and they're getting all sorts of bonuses because they are finding this copywriting talent.

That's the one thing to remember. If you want to get ahead in this industry the people that you want to get in with want to find you as much as you want to find them, and start a relationship with them.

It really comes down to two things as you get going. The first is what we just went over. Forming those relationships, reaching out to those folks in the first place — even if it's completely terrifying — and making the connections.

The second is that you do have to write copy that gets results for your clients. You have to be able to bring in new customers and drive sales. When you can get those results with your copy, then making those relationships continues to be easier and easier.

There's a magic word in the industry. I mentioned it before. It's "control." I've heard stories of great copywriters when they were just getting started getting basically kicked out of offices because they said, "Oh, I want to get started, but I don't have a control."

I think it's gotten a lot easier today than it was then, because you don't even necessarily have to have written a control to get in with some of these big marketers. They can afford to test new writers cheaply online — when they were all doing direct mail, an untested writer was a much bigger risk.

But once you start to have at least one control, where you can say, "Okay I wrote this sales letter, and it got better results than what was working before." Then you're able to get into a lot more places.

Once you can start putting that label of "control" on some of the copy you've written, the doors will open all over the place.

Then you just continue to build those relationships, you continue to get results for clients.

From there if you want to work with the best companies in the industry, you have to adopt the same mindset as the most successful copywriters in the business have. And it's not one where you need to be marketing yourself all the time. It's really one of building relationships and delivering value — and trying to look like you're NOT marketing yourself.

If you're marketing yourself all the time, there are going to be a few questions as to your ability. Because frankly the best copywriters typically don't really have to market themselves — their reputations precede them.

To some degree, yes you do need cash flow. And you may need to more actively do things that don't necessarily look 100% like marketing, but they are still marketing activities. But you can't be seen as marketing yourself all the time.

The best way to do this marketing that doesn't look like marketing is building those relationships. You want to be seen as someone who's courteous and helpful, who is always just connecting with others and helping them connect with other people. These relationships will pay dividends over many years.

I've built relationships with folks for two or three years and then got incredible projects from them. Some will pay off much quicker. Some will say, "Oh, what can you do next month?" But none of that happens until you start connecting.

Be connected with these ideal clients; try and deliver value up front without asking for anything in return.

And delivering value can be simple. Maybe you can offer them a gentle suggestion by simply asking a question like, "Hey, have you tested this idea in a promotion yet?" Or perhaps connecting them with somebody who you think might be valuable to them.

Anything that you can do to deliver value up front is going to continue to build those relationships.

Susan: Do you have a specific process for building those relationships with your ideal clients?

Roy: If you want to break it down to a specific process for getting in with these best companies for marketing yourself, here's what I think you should do…

This is inspired by a process that legendary Madison Avenue Ad Man David Ogilvy actually used. And it's something I've taught my coaching clients to do as well.

First you make a list of all your ideal clients who are already doing the kind of marketing that you want to do. You actually create a spreadsheet with the company, the contact, their phone number or email address or physical mailing address. Everything you need to get in contact with them.

Then you start reaching out to them one by one and focus on building relationships with them. Make them very small, short contacts. A quick email with a question that you think they could answer — and an appreciative "thank you" when they do. A recommendation for a test they could do to improve marketing results. A link to a promo or ad you think they might like to see, from a competitor or someone selling comparable products to their audience. An article you found that made you think of them. Anything they might value, that lets them know you're thinking of them and respect them.

You shouldn't have high hopes on any one of those contacts. When David Ogilvy did this, he had I believe 50 clients on his list, and ended up getting 45 of them over his decades in the advertising business. For me, I have a shorter list than 50, but I occasionally go back to it and see how many more I've checked off the list.

If you just make it a point of making that list of ideal clients, and reaching out to build relationships with them, you'll be blown away by what happens.

I think that's really my best process for working with those best companies and how I've gotten to where I'm at today.

How to Get More Work from Clients You Already Have

Susan: That's great advice. And you've told me how valuable it is to continue building those relationships beyond the first project. What do you suggest for getting more work from clients that you already have?

Roy: If you already have the client, that's great. You're over the first major hurdle.

Frankly, many folks who say that they want to be copywriters don't even get that far — they don't even get one project. And you can't even get started without getting clients in the first place.

However, true success as a copywriter doesn't really come until you are able to generate steady streams of income from clients that you already have.

The first thing that you need to focus on is getting project number two. That's ultimately more important than project number one. Because it represents an ongoing relationship, not a single transaction of, "Okay. I'm going to write a promotion for you."

If you don't get project number two, you're not going to get three, four, five, six, seven, eight, nine, ten either.

Ultimately as a copywriter the real money is made from working multiple times with an individual client, and there are a few reasons for that. As you develop your reputation with them, they're usually willing to pay you more, but also you actually just get to know their products and their market a whole lot better. You get to know their process, so it's smoother, and you can work a lot faster with them.

The longer you have a relationship established with a client, the better you're going to do not only for yourself but for the client. Your marketing will perform better.

The ideal situation is working essentially with the same handful of clients for decades. And you may get some turnover, but with the best clients you'll have almost a partnership status.

In fact, some of the copywriters I know are partners in their clients' businesses. They have an equity stake, and they get paid based on how well the business does. They also have the opportunity to cash out of that equity stake at some point for a very large payday. That's an ideal situation in developing these long-term — even decades-long — relationships.

If you want to do that, yes, you do have to get results. You have to be a good copywriter when it comes to generating new customers and selling again to previous ones. It's also just as important — or possibly more so — to be someone that clients want to work with.

It may sound silly, but really you just have to be a good human being. You have to be someone that they don't dread getting on the phone with to give feedback on your copy. You have to be communicative and nice to them, and all of that is absolutely critical. That's how you're going to end up working with clients on an ongoing basis and really earn a lot more as a copywriter.

It's funny, because I talk a lot about results. And you can't discount how important it is to be able to generate marketing results for your clients. But that's not why they'll keep coming back to you over and over again. They'll keep coming back to you because of the way you make them feel. It's not necessarily a friendship — they are your client, after all — but this human factor is incredibly important.

Show me two copywriters who can write highly-effective copy, and I guarantee the one who is easier to get along with will be more successful in the long run.

Getting Paid: What the Most Financially Successful Copywriters Know

Susan: Very helpful. Now I'd like to turn to compensation structures for copywriters. Can you explain the basics of how copywriters get paid?

Roy: There are a few things that you need to know when it comes to pricing your services and how you actually get paid as a copywriter.

This is called The Copywriter's Guide to Getting Paid for a reason. I want you to be able to earn good money as a copywriter. In order to do that, you have to know the most common ways that copywriters structure their client agreements.

The first and most common agreement you'll see is for a project. You essentially say, "I'm going to do this much work for this amount of money."

This may sound strange if you're used to getting paid an hourly wage, or even a salary.

Yes, there are some clients that insist on paying copywriters on an hourly basis. Very few do it though, unless you're actually an employee. And if a client insists on paying you hourly, I'd recommend you run the other way!

What you want is a client who will pay by the project. Depending on the size of the project, it can be $2,000, $3,000, $10,000, $25,000 or more for the best copywriters to complete a set project. My standard fee as I write this is in the five-figures, for a sales letter and supporting copy. Some projects command even higher fees.

The project itself can take a short period of time. It can take a long period of time. But it's just a flat fee based on the project itself — based on the total deliverables.

As a copywriter you should know that your fee should be big enough that if you don't get paid anything else, that it's going to cover your baseline expenses. That it's going to keep the lights on at your house, it's going to keep your family fed and safe, and you'll have clothes on your back. Your fee should not be what you rely on to get rich — only to cover your expenses.

But it should cover your expenses — relying on royalties to pay your bills is a recipe for disaster. There's just too much that can go wrong — and most of what can go wrong is totally outside of your control.

Because payments are often split 50/50 (50% before and 50% after the project), some copywriters insist on the first 50% being enough to cover expenses. I understand this, and agree to some degree. However I'd like to work with clients who are above board enough that I know I'm going to get both halves of that project fee. If you continuously have clients flake out on you, maybe that's something you need to consider.

That's the project-based fee. Alternately there's the retainer or the salary arrangement. If you're not an employee, it would typically be called a retainer. If you are a taxable employee, it would be called a salary. This is where you get paid on a monthly basis for a certain amount of work.

Some retainers are very small such as, "I need three small things written, and I'm going to pay you based on the value of those three small things."

Some of them are unlimited. You're basically an employee, but you're not actually an employee for tax purposes. They're paying you the retainer to do whatever they ask you to do and to be at their beck and call full-time.

If you have a great client, it's something you should seriously consider if they bring it to you. I know a lot of the clients I work with do want to lock down skilled copywriters. They want to tie that person up, so they can't work for their competitors. And they're willing to pay well for it.

That goes back to what I mentioned before. They need copywriters. They want copywriters. They always want more and better copywriters, and the retainer and salary are available options when you show that you've got the chops.

Susan: You mentioned that you also recommend copywriters get a royalty on top of their fee or retainer. Can you explain a little more about that?

Roy: Absolutely. In the long term, royalties or other pay-for-performance arrangements are the biggest distinguishing factor for whether a copywriter is going to be very successful financially or not. It doesn't matter if you can sell a ton, if you're not getting paid for results, you're going to be making less than you could be and less than you deserve.

Let's run through a few examples of how royalties or pay-for-performance arrangements work.

If it's under pay-for-performance, there can be a bonus based on the number of responses gotten.

This is most common on lead generation projects. If you're doing lead generation it can be a pay-per-lead fee that you set out.

Let's say you're doing lead generation for a high end business service, and their leads are worth $50 to them. Every lead is worth $50 to the company, so you may come up with an arrangement that says, "For every lead that my marketing brings in that's worth $50 to your bottom line, I would like $5 as a commission for bringing that lead in through the door." If you're doing a lot of lead generation, that's a great pay-for-performance metric to base your compensation on.

And then there are royalties — which is where most of my work is done. Royalties are usually calculated as a percentage-of-sales metric.

I very often get at least 5% of the revenue brought in by a promotion. That's typically measured after refunds. If you have a guarantee, a certain number of customers are going to request a refund. I let the client calculate my royalty after the refunds have been taken out of the total revenue number.

My standard arrangement is I get an upfront project fee. That's a fee — it's not an advance of royalties or anything like that. It's a fee that I earn for doing the work, for setting aside time on my schedule. And I also get paid that royalty based on the results that my work generates.

This is something I've really done essentially since the very beginning where all of my projects have been done on a fee plus royalty basis. I've very rarely made any exceptions, and I don't really make exceptions for anybody these days.

In the last 12 months I had to turn down a very good client that I did really want to work with. It happened because despite me repeatedly telling them that this is the only way I work, they wouldn't find a way to pay a royalty or performance bonus for the work they wanted me to do. So in the end, I simply refused to do work for them.

Ultimately, if you're a direct response copywriter who writes copy with a measurable result — whether that's lead generation, actually generating sales, or any other measurable action — you should be paid based on the success you create for your client. Find out a way to measure that value to your client, and come to an arrangement where you get paid on those results.

I think you should absolutely charge a fee simply to set aside the time to do the work. And your royalty or pay-for-performance bonus should come above and beyond that. It's the way the best copywriters in the business get paid, and it's the way you should get paid too, if you want to make a great living at this.

Secrets to Successful Self-Promotion for Copywriters

Susan: Okay, so we've talked about getting paid. Now let's talk about getting clients. What are the best ways for copywriters to promote themselves?

Roy: Honestly, I never felt like I've been that good at self-promotion, except for the one thing I do really well.

I just continuously introduce myself to ideal clients, whether it's an email or LinkedIn message or whatever, sent to the clients that I would love to work with. I'm always trying to form relationships with them. Combine that with my relentless focus on developing the ability to get results. That one-two punch has really gotten me all the work that I can handle.

In the short term if you're a brand new copywriter, finding specs or doing the irresistible offer letter I mentioned before (and that you can read in Appendix A) are great ideas. Those are perfect ways to get in the door as a copywriter.

That's just getting started. But before long, you will have done a couple of projects and you'll have a little bit out there you can point to and say, "Look I did that, it was successful."

That's when I think you need to come up with a short list of ideal companies to work with, and connect with them. Become known to them, and become somebody who's on their radar. Stay in contact with them in a friendly non-pestering manner.

I spent some time in sales, before I became a freelance copywriter. One particular product I was selling had a long sales cycle — it often took weeks or months to close the deal. Once I had my first couple of conversations with a prospect, my next contacts were often as simple as a short one or two sentence email saying, "Hey is there anything else that I can help you with right now to move your purchasing process forward?" That is far more appealing and far more likely to get you a response than trying to be "salesy."

If you think of it like a relationship, you're going to communicate with these prospective clients like a real human you want to build a relationship with. And that's what's most effective. (That's a lesson both for building your copywriting business and for your actual copywriting.)

Translating that to your copywriting business, you might write a potential client and say, "Is there anything that I can help you with right now? Do you have any upcoming projects that I might be able to help you with? Or is there any other way I can be of service?" That's far more likely to get you a response than almost anything else you can do in terms of marketing.

These are all very solid strategies for getting connected and getting projects in the next few weeks or the next few months.

Susan: And what about for the long-term?

Roy: If you want to establish yourself for the longer term, the number one thing that you need to do is become a recognized expert in your field. For this, your approach to marketing and self-promotion are very different. You need to be somebody that folks in your small circle, in your industry, will recognize.

Usually that involves publishing. Doing a book, doing a blog, writing articles for great publications or industry websites — this is just a starter list, but it's a good one. The idea is that you want to be present anywhere that you'll be seen by your industry.

Doing videos on YouTube is another example, getting in front of your ideal prospects with a video or other way of featuring your expertise will help. Also, creating products that establish your expertise is an incredible way to build authority and to become a recognized expert.

Speaking is another great way to establish instant credibility. Find a way to speak in front of whomever your main set of prospects are. Getting on that stage is something most folks are deathly afraid of — and as a result they assign tremendous power and authority to folks who do it. It will instantly elevate your credibility.

These are all mechanical suggestions. It's also important what you're saying and writing about in these places.

You need to think about how you can be known for getting results. Direct response marketers and businesses in general who are sensitive to their numbers will be naturally attracted to your message of being able to generate sales and profits. This is the altar at which they all pray.

I keep coming back to this because it's so important. When you can consistently generate sales, you will forever be in demand with these ideal clients. When you're putting together your book or articles or speeches or whatever, find a way to make them case studies of what you did and the incredible results it got. This is a one-two punch that will make you incredibly attractive to clients willing to pay you a lot of money.

Along the way, make sure you're always building your marketing chops. Not just your ability to generate sales for yourself, but for your clients.

It's an absolute necessity — especially if you're fairly new to being a copywriter. This isn't about getting projects right now, but it's the most effective form of self-promotion we have.

Focus on becoming a great copywriter. Learn the advanced strategies of direct response that you can use to create winning promotions and sales letters and advertisements more often.

It doesn't sound like a way to promote yourself. But the better you are in getting results for your clients, the more promotion you're doing indirectly.
Because if you do a piece of advertising that gets noticed by the industry, then everybody is going to want to figure out who you are.

How Some Copywriters Earn 100X What Others Do

Susan: Excellent, now you wanted to talk about some of the other opportunities copywriters have to get paid — can you explain?

Roy: There's a couple that I think are great.

I guess the first one that I should mention is what I did in the very beginning. If you are new to copywriting and you just want an income and maybe benefits and the potential for growth and learning, then getting a job is not a bad thing to do. It can be a bridge toward becoming a freelancer.

Maybe that means working for one of the major direct marketers. Or it may involve working for a small business and taking a larger role in their marketing.

The major direct marketers hire in-house copywriters, and that's both a great training ground and an instant reputation booster. For example, having worked for an Agora division is an almost instant "in" with many clients in the industry. There are many big direct marketing companies who hire in-house copywriters. Some will require you to work in-office — which also means moving if you're not in their city. But some will let you work from home, as long as you're responsive to their needs and not using working from home as an excuse to goof off.

It can also be a great opportunity to work for a small business. You can end up running a marketing department, writing copy, and doing a lot of other things just like I did. That can also be a further learning ground for your marketing and copywriting abilities.

Usually working in a small business does require you to be more self-directed. You'll have to spearhead the implementation of direct response strategies. If you're not dealing with a boss or business owner that's oriented toward direct response, sometimes testing new approaches can be challenging. But with the right attitude, there can be a ton of opportunity in this approach. And if you're getting results, that will speak for itself.

There are also gigs you can get in ad agencies, bigger companies, and other job-type environments. At the risk of sweeping generalities, most of these are institutionally opposed to direct response. If you want to measure your effectiveness and get paid based on results, you're unlikely to find those opportunities here. I generally recommend copywriters with their mind set on direct response avoid these situations in favor of actual direct response companies or more entrepreneurial companies in general.

The second opportunity for copywriters to get paid is in actually creating their own business. You're actually walking the walk using your own copy to sell products or services — and I'm not talking about your copywriting business here.

I did this with my dad very early in my marketing journey. He had recorded a video about how to cut foam wings for model airplanes. He uses a fairly innovative method, and the video was full of valuable content.

He'd been selling it on eBay, but sales tapered off. So I said, "Let's set up a website, and I'll write all the copy and create all the marketing for it." It worked. It hasn't made us a fortune because it's a tiny little market. But it's generated thousands of dollars over the past few years that we wouldn't have had otherwise, and it also taught me a lot about running my own marketing system.

Doing something like this can create an ongoing and consistent revenue stream. It can help you better understand the total marketing process. It could even become your main thing. You could tap into something and end up saying, "Jeez, why did I ever want to be a copywriter when I can use my copywriting skills to make so much more money in my own business?"

I hear many veteran freelance copywriters looking back at their career and wishing they had created their own business. Instead of working for five cents on the dollar in terms of royalties earned, maybe they could have earned the 30% profit margin that their client is earning on the same marketing campaign, or even better.

Alternately, I think as you develop your skills, you should look at opportunities to become a partner in a business. If you find an opportunity that makes a lot of sense for you, you can offer your marketing skills and work in exchange for equity in the business. You can become a founding partner in a new business, and run the marketing. Frankly the richest copywriters that I know have all done this, and this is something that I'm personally interested in moving more and more towards.

This model would require an entire book by itself, so we won't go too deep into it. But you should know this is an alternate opportunity to get paid a LOT more as a copywriter.

How Much Money Can a Good Copywriter Make?

Susan: Roy, how much money can a good copywriter make?

Roy: There's no ceiling to this. Here are some very rare examples, and these should not be expected, but rather give you a glimpse as to what's possible.

One good example is Gary Bencivenga. He's considered to be the world's best copywriter — though it's folks like Brian Kurtz from Boardroom heaping on this praise, because Gary never says these things about himself.

Gary wrote one promotion for one client that mailed profitably over 100 million times in the mid 1990's. He was earning a royalty of five cents per piece mailed on this promotion. Which means, if you do the math, that's essentially 5% of that 100 million or $5 million for something which took him maybe three or four months of work. That was the royalty. If you become very good at copywriting, it really becomes a "sky is the limit" opportunity.

Alternately, if you become a partner in a business that becomes a $10 million business, a $50 million business, $100 million business, what does it mean to cash out that equity stake? Or even just consider the ongoing income from owning a piece of the business.

My first "sky is the limit" experience was that first $1 million promo I did. That promo generated over $1 million in revenue. It was sent out online over about two weeks. It was a very short period of time where I generated that revenue. I earned a 3.5% royalty on that — 3.5% of $1 million is $35,000. And that was on top of my fee. Of course, having just made over $1 million, the client was happy to write that check!

This is something where a few weeks of work can earn you as much in royalty as the average American family earns in a year.

Of course, these are exceptions and not every copywriter will earn fees or royalties like that. If you cut it down to the average for everybody who ever bought a book on copywriting or a program on copywriting, the average is going to be much lower. Because there are a lot of people who don't dedicate themselves to starting with that first project, becoming successful, then doing a second project, and a third project, and a fourth project, and continuing to go on and develop themselves over years and decades to get really, really, really good at this. That's what the folks who become off the charts earners as copywriters have done.

In the short term, I was able to get a very good salary when I had zero marketing experience just by doing decent studying on marketing and being focused on doing what it would take to be successful. I at least doubled, maybe tripled my income within four or five years with that company. When I went on my own as a freelancer, I quickly made up that income and just continued beating my income goals.

It's a great way to earn a living. I work part time from home, I pick up my kids from school when they're done many days of the week. There's a lot of flexibility, and it's a great lifestyle that if you're serious about it, it can pay some very large rewards.

Roy's #1 Rule for Success

Susan: That's so exciting. How do you want to wrap this up? Do you have any final words for these guys?

Roy: Yes. Number one, you must take action. When it all comes down to it, it can't be a dream. It can't be something you imagine for yourself as happening some time out in the future — because that will never come.

You need to do something today. You need to take action today to get started, to get that first project out of the way. You're going to fail, and it may be miserably, but you need to do it. And then you need to get your second and your third and your fourth and your fifth project out of the way and just keep going and building momentum.

For the potential clients that you're not even doing projects with yet, you need to be creating relationships with them. The better your relationships are today, the better opportunities you're going to have tomorrow. You need to focus on creating those relationships.

Then finally you do need to get very good at writing copy that makes sales if you want to be a well-paid copywriter. Especially if you want to be a direct response copywriter that does very well for yourself, and that's able to get access to and create all these opportunities. You absolutely need to focus on developing your skills as a copywriter and marketer in addition to developing your career and your copywriting business.

Learn as you go. Just get started. Nike struck on an eternal success truth of the universe with their slogan, "Just do it." And as you're doing it, make sure you're always learning and developing your skills.

You do need to focus on finding the best teachers that you can find, who can help you take your skills to the next level. That's part of what I try to do at Breakthrough Marketing Secrets. There are a lot of places to learn, but it's something that the best copywriters spend their entire career doing: getting better as they build their business.

If folks are interested in following my writing, they can certainly sign up at the Breakthrough Marketing Secrets website at www.BreakthroughMarketingSecrets.com. They'll continue to get my best insight and experience on business, marketing, selling, and copywriting — both the craft and the business.

Susan: Very good. I want to thank you, Roy, for sharing your copywriting success story with us and allowing us to peek behind the curtain on what really works. I think it's been very enlightening. Thank you.

Roy: Absolutely. Thanks Susan.

Appendix A — How to Get Your First Copywriting Client

One of the most common questions I get is, "Roy, how do you get your FIRST copywriting client?"

I know how it goes…

You've been doing all that book learnin' — and now you're rarin' to go!

You've heard of the untold riches that copywriters can earn — and you want your share!

But there's a big gap…

(And this is the SAME gap that exists with almost any other job.)

Clients want a copywriter with experience. But you can't get experience without getting that first client.

What is an aspiring copywriter to do?!

Well, I've written before about the value of an irresistible offer…

And that's EXACTLY what you need to do…

You need to find YOUR perfect client to get started with… And make them an offer they simply can't refuse! (No horse heads required!)

My story…

Rewind to August 2006. I'd gotten my first "real" marketing job more than a year beforehand, and was still working that full-time.

I'd wanted to become a freelance copywriter since I'd discovered direct response marketing, before I'd landed that marketing gig. But I'd had it too good, and been too busy in the marketing job, to go after clients.

But I'd been following this guy named David Bullock for a while.

He was one of Perry Marshall's "gurus" — and he taught an advanced form of marketing testing called "Taguchi."

He had a high-end course on the market that was a major brain dump of everything he knew about Taguchi, testing design, and how to use this advanced testing methodology as an entrepreneur.

I'm a bit of a geek when it comes to this stuff, so I was interested.

And as a rabid direct marketer from the word "go," I knew the power of testing — so I was doubly-interested.

Anyway, I got to know David's work a bit, and had even contacted him and reached out to him a few months before.

But that had gone nowhere.

I wasn't satisfied though, so I used the copywriting skills I'd been developing to — this is a SHOCKER — write him a sales letter!

And here's the exact letter I sent (via email)...

David, I challenge you to a duel...

David,

I have to admit, I'm disappointed... in myself.

You see, when we talked back in May, I had you convinced that I had copywriting skills you could use. And that your clients could use. But I made a mistake that you--an experienced salesman--will easily recognize.

I failed to follow up. Once I'd confirmed your interest, I'd assumed I'd made the sale. Now that three months have passed with no collaboration, I'm sure I've fallen to the back of your mind. But that's a filthy place to be, so...

I'm going to come out kicking and screaming to convince you to pull me back to the front of your mind...

To earn my spot in the front of your mind, I have an "incredible offer" for you. Now, I know that as thinking people we're taught to distrust this type of deal. But as emotional people--we love 'em. You can decide for yourself that you're going to love my deal.

(Here's my moment's hesitation thinking I'm crazy challenging an ad optimization specialist to a duel!)

As one of the world's foremost authorities on ad testing, I'm sure you're familiar with the phrase "beat the control."

Well, that's exactly what I'd like to do. Completely at my risk.

I hereby challenge your sales letter located at [URL] to a duel!

I'll create a challenger... a letter to take on your control in an A/B split test. I'll do my research, write the sales letter, and present it to you to review. If you don't like it, you tell me it's junk and file it directly into your wastebasket. If you think it might do better than your control, you test it. If at any point during the test it looks like my letter performs worse than your control, pull it and declare your control the winner.

The best part for you is that through this point, you risk only one thing...

That my challenger will be successful and that you'll have to pay me for my hard work. If you didn't like my letter, you didn't even test it then you owe me nothing. If you thought it might work but it flopped instead, you still owe me nothing.

Even if the response to my challenger is just a hair under your control, plus it gives you ideas you apply on your own to make your control pull even better... you still owe me nothing!

My challenger will only be declared a winner after it proves, in testing, that it gives you more conversions and higher profits than your control. So really...

I'm offering to risk my time and energy to increase your sales, while you risk nothing but higher profits.

Sounds pretty good, huh?

So what's my reward? If my letter does beat your control, I expect fair compensation. Based on the price point of the products, and that they are information products (which have notoriously high margins), I propose that a fair prize for this duel is $5000.

If you accept the terms of this "beat the control" duel, please notify me immediately. I will send you my address, so you can ship a copy of your complete package. Once I receive the product, I will study it thoroughly so that I can write a letter to your prospects that explains, in detail, all the ways they will benefit by purchasing it from you.

Within 60 days from receiving your package, I will deliver this letter to you, for you to decide to test it. On your schedule, but in no more than 30 days, you will let me know if you have decided to test the letter. Within 120 days after that, you will update me on the status of the test.

If, after thorough testing, my challenger does beat your control... making it clear that it will bring you increased conversions and increased profits... payment will be due within 30 days from the date the outcome of the A/B test is decided. But wait...

By studying your system in order to write a sales letter for it, I will have thorough knowledge of Taguchi testing...

How it works... How to apply it in ad testing... How to use it to take a good thing and make it better. If my letter beats your control, becoming your new control, you may want my help making it even better through thorough testing and tweaking. So here's my "icing on the cake" offer...

As long as my letter stays your control... as long as it holds up against any letter that challenges it... I will provide consultation and copywriting services related to the letter at a discounted rate of $75/hour... half the $150/hour I'd charge for similar work if I were to get it today.

That means next week you'd pay just $75/hour to develop test conditions. Next year, same rate. Even in 4 years, if my control is still fending off all opposition, continuing to make you profits, and I've raised my rates to $400/hour... but you want my consultation on what we could plug into the test to make the letter pull better... you'll still get everything short of a complete and total rewrite at $75/hour. Not a bad deal... don't you think?

Reply now to take advantage of this "incredible offer"...

To have a control-bustin', sales-makin', profit-increasin', duel-winnin' sales letter written for you without any risk on your part.

Just reply to this e-mail to let me know that you accept the terms of the duel, and I'll send you my address so we can get started right away.

Yours for the challenge,

Roy

P.S. - Direct response advertising tradition states that I should use the P.S. to remind you that there is no risk on your part. You only pay for my control-bustin' letter after it's proven that it outperforms your control. (And that only after you decided that it's up to your standards to test.)

To get most professional copywriters to challenge your control, you'd have to pay at least $5000 up front, just to get them to write the letter. And there'd be no guarantee of results.

By asking you to pay me only if my letter brings you increased conversions and increased profits, you have no risk but to increase your profits. So act now by hitting reply and telling me that you accept.

As you can probably guess, David said... "Yes!"

(And I beat his control.)

Now here's a moment of warning...

Don't chase down David yourself. He'll hate me and he'll hate you if I spur a bunch of imitators trying to go to HIM. (He does very little with Taguchi anymore anyway — a subject for another day.)

Instead, do what a smart copywriter does. Study this. Take it apart. Really work to understand the offer — and what makes it so irresistible. And then, without looking at the original letter, write your own version, to your own ideal client.

WARNING:

Doing this will cause you to sweat bullets.

It will be incredibly uncomfortable to press the "send" button. And even more uncomfortable after you've already done so.

And then you'll wait with baited breath, in the hope you'll get the call back.

This is all a natural part of the process. Read my past article "Be scared shitless" for encouragement. (It's Appendix E in this book.)

Doing this has opened all sorts of doors for me.

This was my first copywriting client, and it's led me to get "warm" connections with so many of the greats of the marketing world. It started the ball rolling on my copywriting career. It got the "first" out of the way so I could get my second and third and fourth and so on copywriting clients.

David and I are still friends to this day.

And it's in no small part because of this offer I made to him.

Now here's my final lesson you can take away, no matter what business you're in…

Whether you're a copywriter looking for your first client, or simply your next…

Whether you're a business owner in an unrelated niche, just looking to sell more of your products or services…

No matter what business or industry you're in…

You need to study irresistible offers!

Here's a little secret. Finding the right audience for your sales message is 40% of its success. The offer you make is another 40%. And what you say — while important — only accounts for about 20% of your total success.

Which means if you understand offers... And sending them to the right people... You're 80% of the way to getting the success you want.

Think how YOU can create an irresistible offer on your next project.

What can you do to make saying "no" harder than saying "YES!" as I did for David?

And sit down and write an open, honest, heartfelt letter making an offer so irresistible and weighted to your prospect that you're sweating bullets when you hit send...

And watch how fast they get in contact with you.

Appendix B — How and Why to Get an Awesome Marketing Job

I previously wrote about how to get your first copywriting client. In that article, I shared the exact formula I used to land my first freelance gig with a respected marketing expert.

But a little more than a year before that, I'd actually landed a full-time marketing gig…

If you're an aspiring copywriter or marketer with zero experience in marketing…

I can't recommend this strongly enough!

I don't know how many times it's come in handy that I have real, in-the-trenches marketing experience ON TOP OF pretty good copywriting skills…

But I can tell you this…

I don't know a single highly-successful copywriter today who doesn't understand the intricacies of the ENTIRE marketing department…

Even if all they do 99.9% of the time is hole themselves up in their basement office and crank out high-octane sales copy.

Because…

Sales copy doesn't exist in a vacuum!

It's certainly important.

It can make or break a campaign.

But there are MANY moving pieces in an effective marketing campaign. And if you get ONE wrong, your response can go KAPUT!

And so as a copywriter, your services, insight, and contributions can MULTIPLY in VALUE (along with your fees) if you understand the big picture of marketing.

And that's why I absolutely, positively recommend without reservation…

You should "quit" your dream of The Writer's Life…

… And get a REAL JOB!

Listen, I appreciate that you want all the perks of being a freelance copywriter…

- Working from home, or anywhere!

- Control of your schedule, and no boss to get all bossy on you!

- And near-unlimited earning potential!

And yet, it may pay — in the long-run — to get a "real" 9-to-5 marketing job that puts you in the trenches in an established company, responsible for MANY aspects of marketing.

Getting leads. Converting leads. Managing email marketing programs. Digging into your database and uncovering additional profit opportunities. Driving referrals. Keeping a website up. And so on.

If it's NOT a direct response company, but you can use ROI-minded marketing to help them grow, that's great. (This is what I did, more than doubling the company in under 5 years, and earning them a spot on Inc. Magazine's list of America's Fastest-Growing Private Businesses.)

If you can get an in-house gig at an established direct marketing company, that's great too. If you've got ambition, there will most likely be at least one (if not many) key players in the company who are willing to feed your ambition and success through mentorship… Knowing you're helping their company grow.

Either way, you'll be growing hugely valuable skills!

The better you understand every aspect of marketing, the better you can help all your future clients develop effective marketing strategies and systems.

And you will have intimate knowledge of all those pieces and parts…

Which means you'll know exactly what every piece of sales copy needs to do…

And the best way to do it!

PLUS you'll be getting paid to learn!

So let's say you have ZERO experience but you want to land an awesome marketing job…

How do you do it?

The exact same way I did!

One look at my resume in the mid-2000s would have said I was severely under-qualified to take over a marketing department.

But I couldn't respond to a "help wanted" ad without sending my resume…

So I hid it beneath a cover letter that essentially said…

(And I'm sorry I can't dig up the original right now — it's at least two computers ago, and perhaps lost to the ages…)

Dear XYZ,

I'm writing in response to your ad for a Marketing Manager position.

If you take a moment to look at my resume, you'll think — no doubt — that I'm not qualified for the job at all.

I'd like the opportunity to prove that assumption wrong.

First, I'd like to highlight my experience at XXX. While this wasn't a marketing job, it gave me XXX skills that are directly relevant because XXX.

Also my experience at YYY will help me achieve success with your company because YYY.

[Fill in more experience here.]

Not only that, you'll find that I'll work both harder and smarter than any other candidate for the position, simply because I want it more.

While I may not have much direct marketing experience on my resume, I've become an avid student of effective and proven marketing strategies, and would like the opportunity to work with you to apply them in your business.

Let's talk. You can get a hold of me at ### or by email at XXX@example.com.

Sincerely,

YOUR NAME

You may be starting to recognize a theme…

It's another irresistible offer!

There are very few job candidates who will ever send a letter like this. It shows at least some marketing chops. And they'll absolutely want to speak with you.

You'll still have to prove yourself in the interview, and on the job.

But this letter is a HUGE first step to getting in the door. Don't swipe it word-for-word. Capture the idea in your own voice. Make it relevant to your potential employer.

My old boss repeatedly told me that he never would have considered me on my resume alone. But with that cover letter, I got through the golden gates, and became a member of the company's "brain trust."

It was also a huge training ground where I was able to develop many of the proven marketing skills I have today.

And a success story — as we more than doubled their business in my time there.

If you're looking to get good at marketing or copywriting, you should not write off getting a "real" job for a while.

I promise, it'll be worth it.

Appendix C — What Makes a Perfect Copywriting Client

9 Criteria of a Perfect Copywriting Client

If you're a copywriter, you need to know one of the most important factors to your success is the quality of your clients. Better clients means better opportunities. Better marketing used around your copy. Higher fees and higher royalties, plus a client that's happy to pay them. You'll get better feedback on what you write, and develop your skills faster and to higher heights. You can't go wrong getting better clients.

If you hire copywriters, making yourself one of the best clients out there will attract the best copywriting talent available. The best copywriters will only work with the best clients. There's too much opportunity cost in doing anything less. And so you need to become one of these ideal clients.

This would all be platitudes if it didn't come with a specific list. And that's coming.

But first, let's answer this question…

What makes a perfect copywriting client?

Well, the goal of a copywriter is to work as little as possible for as much income as possible. (Isn't that the case for everybody?)

Sure, great copywriters will outwork 99.9% of the people on the planet. But they only want to do so when the rewards are worth it. They want maximum return for time invested. And they're sharp about it — with enough years' experience behind you; you can start to figure out where your time and effort will be rewarded, and where it will not.

And so great copywriters are looking for certain markers of what makes a great client. What is consistent about those businesses that lead to maximum income in minimum time, and with minimum hassle? And why are those things important?

My personal experience…

I've been developing my list of criteria for about as long as I've been in marketing. I know what makes a good business — and in particular, a good direct response business.

Things like list size, the use of my kind of direct marketing, good products and customer experience, and so on.

I'd even kept a bit of a list in the back of my head, based on these concepts. But I'd never formalized them.

Until I was recently listening to a Clayton Makepeace recording, where he rattled off his list of…

9 Criteria for a Perfect Copywriting Client!

Is this list exhaustive? No. But it's a pretty darn good one.

And I've always made myself and my clients more money by following Clayton's advice. So I took Clayton's ideas and fleshed them out in my own words.

The list you see below was originally written to potential clients and partners, and only minimally edited here.

This gives you a gist of what you need to be looking for in finding that "perfect" client. Or becoming the perfect client, if you're the one doing the hiring.

Here's the list...

1. Products that deliver what they promise... I'm NOT interested in working with shysters, hucksters, or peddlers of snake oil. You MUST have a quality product and customer experience. Otherwise, better marketing will make you fail faster — whether that's getting shacked up with Bubba, or simply getting exposed on RipoffReport or some similar consumer-advocate review site (one or two bad reviews don't concern me — there's always somebody — but teeming masses of dissatisfaction are trouble I don't wish to confront).

2. A copy-centric culture... Long copy sells. If we have to have this argument, we're not a fit. Period. However, if you believe in "The Primacy of Copy" and have a history of using long copy (in whatever media) to sell your products, we might be a fit...

3. Sizable customer list... I want to help already successful businesses become way MORE successful... While I love the idea of helping a startup find their footing and experience massive success... I know the reality is not all roses. But if you've proven that a market exists and you're able to sell into it successfully... Well, there are at least a dozen ways I can help you achieve more success, faster.

4. Demonstrated list growth... The absolute WORST thing that can happen to an effective marketing campaign is to have it sit on the shelf, collecting dust. I want to know that you're already working to grow your file before me, and if I create highly-effective marketing for you, that you'll invest in putting it into the market.

5. A testing obsession... Good direct marketing is testing. Period. Yes, your experience matters. But good and bad marketing are not decided in a conference room. They are decided in the marketplace. And the only votes that matter are the customers' — and the only way they cast their vote is with their wallet. Test... Test... Test!

6. A "Fail Fast" attitude... Money loves speed. A client who spends 8 months trying to get "the one" campaign just right is a fool. A client who tests a new campaign every 1-2 months (maybe more often) to find what works best, is smart. This is not an excuse for sloppiness or inept approaches. However you MUST be dedicated to getting new promotions into the market fast, seeing if they work, and planning future action accordingly.

7. Smart marketing managers... What this really means is that the key people within your business MUST be dedicated to the principles of direct marketing, largely outlined here. They must have an attitude that supports business growth, effective client acquisition, and profit maximization. If someone is in a key role and they do not support this, proper action must be taken — first redirection, then replacement if necessary.

8. Fair compensation structure... The late Marty Edelston, the founder of Boardroom, Inc., didn't consider it a good year unless he was paying his top copywriters MORE than he took home as the owner of the business. While I won't use this as a measuring stick, this is the attitude you need to have. If 12 months from now my marketing has doubled your customer base and tripled your profits, you should be ecstatic to have paid me accordingly.

9. A reputation for paying in full — and fast!
Waiting around for late checks to arrive doesn't engender trust or liking. And those are keys to a successful partnership.

Well, there ya go.

Next time you're lining up with a potential client, think about these criteria. Formulate questions to help you evaluate them as you talk through the possibility of working together.

It'll be hard to find a 100% fit...

The "perfect" client probably doesn't exist. They're still a client, after all. But if you find a client who hits 7 or 8 of 9, you're going to be in pretty dang good shape. And by simply testing them against this list, you may find a red flag BEFORE it becomes a problem, NOT AFTER.

Knowing who to turn away will also be incredibly beneficial. Bad clients can suck up time, energy, and motivation. They can ruin your week, your month, your year. You don't need that.

The earlier you can pinpoint who will be a bad client and why, the better off you'll be. If their shortcomings will be a minor annoyance, you can insulate against them as much as possible at the start of the relationship. If the shortcomings are major, you can move on faster.

And for clients...

You can use this list to develop a business that attracts star copywriters who can write profitable promotion after profitable promotion; the ones that can bring floods of new customers through the door, and generate piles of profits from your house file. This is your blueprint. Ignore it at your peril.

Appendix D — My Response to a Copywriter Looking for Career Advice

From time to time I get copywriters approaching me for career advice.

I recently, for example, set up a coaching/copy chief arrangement with a copywriter, and helped her score a big opportunity with one of the major financial publishers. (She had the right attitude: she paid first, asked for advice after.)

And then there's a guy who has emailed me a few times over the last few years asking for advice. And I've been a sucker and spent a little bit of time emailing back and forth each time. (I'm becoming more of a curmudgeon about this — don't think about it unless you're willing to pay my hourly consulting fees.)

So he comes around again in the last few weeks, asking for more advice.

Turns out he hasn't done much of anything I recommended before, but it still bugs him that he's not yet living "The Writer's Life" and earning six-figures as a copywriter.

And now he's questioning whether or not it's worth spending an hour on the phone with me to get his questions answered.

Without saying it directly, he's asking me if spending an hour on the phone with me will give him, 1) guaranteed entry into the high-paying direct response copywriting world, and 2) guaranteed six-figure income… Which he broke down to $8,500 per month.

Listen, I get that you want it.

I get that it's what you've been promised.

And I know for a fact it's friggin' real.

Those of us in the hallowed halls of direct response copywriting are NOT making it up.

However, you're NOT going to get it just by buying an hour of my time, or buying a copywriting course (even the good ones), or anything other than dogged determination and hard work.

Okay, here's the email...

And he was nervous about "airing his laundry in public" so I have made sure that NOTHING in here is personally identifiable...

[REDACTED],

My response to your email will not be what you want. But it will be what you need.

What you're asking me for is a magic pill or magic button that will get you instant copywriting success. You're not going to get that by changing industries. You're not going to get that in an hour on the phone with me. You're not going to get that in this email, either.

And as long as you're focused on the money you get instead of the value you create and provide you're never going to get it.

I read this on the first of every month: http://www.cracked.com/blog/6-harsh-truths-that-will-make-you-better-person/ You would be well-served by reading it frequently and internalizing its "harsh truths."

Eminem's recent song Rap God has a line I have pasted on my wall, "Full of myself, but still hungry, I bully myself 'cause I make me do what I put my mind to, and I'm a million leagues above you."

Without fail, the most successful people I know bully themselves. They don't talk about it. You won't find it in a self-help book, because it's not an idea that the magic pill buyers want to buy. But from time to time they'll let a line slip that talks about how hard they are on themselves.

You need to make yourself do the work.

Study the masters, old and new. Learn the industry yourself. Nothing I can tell you in an email or an hour or a year will matter — you have to learn, I can't teach.

Learn to sell. Get an in-person sales job. I used to sell newspaper subscriptions in grocery stores. I've also sold credit cards, appliance repair plans, IT training solutions, nonprofit donations, and more. Apply those principles in writing.

Do your own homework. If you rely on someone to do it for you, you will never earn six figures in this biz.

There are people in all sorts of industries earning six-figures from copywriting. I'm certain there are at least a few copywriters in your niche earning six figures, doing the same kind of work you insist you can't earn six-figures on. The grass is always greener, my friend. Until you get there. You can either waste your life looking for greener pastures, or you can cultivate the one you're in. You do that by focusing on providing real value, and not being caught up in "How can I create the six-figure writer's life dream for myself?" It'll come if you're doing the right things. But spending all day obsessing about that is not the right thing.

Folks in the direct response field earn six-figures because of RESULTS generated.

You want to make $8,500 per month? I'll show you the fastest, easiest way to do it.

First, find a client who will pay you 3% royalties on sales generated. Most beginning copywriters can get that. Then, find a way to make them $283,333 per month in sales. If you can get them to agree to a 5% royalty, simply make them $170,000 per month. They will be ecstatic to pay you $8,500 per month. You want to make twice as much? Make your clients twice as much.

If I want to make $1 million from a single piece of sales copy — which is my next big goal — I know how to do it. If I'm working for a client, I simply have to write a piece of sales copy that generates $20 million in sales at a 5% royalty. Notice, my focus is not on my $1 million. It's on how I can make my client $20 million. They'll be happy to write me that check for $1 million after that. And I will have earned it.

It's not easy. Most direct response copywriters spend their first 5 or so years still really learning their chops and getting experience. They spend their next 5 getting really good. And those who manage to stick that out spend the rest of their careers getting rich. Even the legends — Gary Bencivenga, Gary Halbert, Dan Kennedy, Eugene Schwartz, (and so on, and so on) — went through this same process. Me and all the writers you mentioned are NOT new to this game, either. We've all had our learning curves. We all stuck with it. And all of us feel like we're just getting started...

I'm not going to tell you anything more helpful in an hour on the phone than what I've just told you now.

If you take this to heart and use it, and change your mind about this whole thing, this email will be worth that six-figures you're looking for. If you don't, well, there's nothing else I can do for you.

Wishing you the best,

Roy Furr

There you have it. The secret to earning six-figures (or even $1 million!) while living the writer's lifestyle as a freelance copywriter.

Or you can apply the same skills and start your own business. There's even more opportunity in doing that! And if you want to make a fortune starting your own business, I have a magic easy button to sell you... All you have to do is push it before you go to bed tonight and you'll wake up rich tomorrow. I swear.

Or you can get real about what it takes to be successful in business and marketing... Just keep reading Breakthrough Marketing Secrets.

Appendix E — Be Scared Shitless

This is going to sound like bragging. If you get caught up in that, you're missing the point.

When I started out my life as a freelance copywriter, I managed to land all the gigs others wanted.

My first freelance client was David Bullock. David is one of the world's leading authorities on Taguchi testing — the most sophisticated, advanced method of testing your marketing.

My second freelance client was Ken McCarthy. Ken was the FIRST person in the world to host an internet marketing seminar, in 1994 in Silicon Valley. His System Seminar in the early 2000s was where nearly every internet marketing guru today got their chops.

I've worked with the world's top trainer of copywriters, AWAI. With the world's most-recognized motivational and personal development products publisher, Nightingale-Conant. With a handful of others in that space.

And in the financial world — where I've worked for the past few years — I've worked with many of the top players in the biz. I've sat across the table from financial and investment gurus that would make most stumble, stammer, and drool. I've had drinks with partners in banks, and interviewed owners of companies that are worth billions.

I've worked directly with marketers who have billions' of dollars in sales to their name.

I email back and forth with nationally-recognized entrepreneurs and marketers — and they happily pick up the phone when they see my name on the caller ID.

Heck, I never even should have been hired for my very first marketing job. I had literally no relevant experience. My degree was in psychology — not marketing or business.

It's not an accident that all of these things happen.

It's not a fluke.

And it's certainly not something that ONLY I am capable of.

When I started out, I didn't have an "in" with any of these people.

I had one thing.

I had the willingness to be scared shitless.

And then, in the middle of all that fear, take action anyway.

I'd make first contact with many of these folks with sweating palms and trembling voice.

But I'd do it. Most people won't.

If you want more success than most people will ever experience, you have to do things, take steps, and find resources that most people never will.